SCIENCE 610
The Earth and the Universe

INTRODUCTION |3

1. PLANT AND ANIMAL SYSTEMS 5

PLANT SYSTEMS |6
ANIMAL AND HUMAN SYSTEMS |11
GENETICS AND REPRODUCTION |19
ECOLOGICAL SYSTEMS |22
SELF TEST 1 |25

2. CHEMISTRY AND PHYSICS 28

MATTER |29
LIGHT |32
SOUND |35
MOTION |36
SELF TEST 2 |38

3. SPACESHIP EARTH AND THE STARS 40

EARTH'S ROTATION |41
EARTH'S ORBIT |43
ECLIPSES OF THE SUN AND MOON |44
OUR SOLAR SYSTEM |45
BRIEF HISTORY OF ASTRONOMY |48
THE STARS |50
MAGNITUDE AND LUMINOSITY |50
SELF TEST 3 |52

LIFEPAC Test is located in the center of the booklet, as well as a Periodic Table for reference. Please remove before starting the unit.

Author:
Barry G. Burrus, M.Div., M.A., B.S.

Editors:
Alpha Omega Staff

Illustrations:
Brian Ring/Alpha Omega Staff

MEDIA CREDITS:
Pages 5: © Eraxion, iStock, Thinkstock; **28:** © Marcochow, iStock, Thinkstock; **32:** © leonello, iStock, Thinkstock; **35:** © danefromspain, iStock, Thinkstock; **36:** © DigitalStorm, iStock, Thinkstock; **40:** © NASA, Bill Anders; **48:** Top, © James Steidl, iStock, Thinkstock; Bottom, © NASA, Goddard Space Flight Center.

Alpha Omega
PUBLICATIONS

804 N. 2nd Ave. E.
Rock Rapids, IA 51246-1759

The Earth and the Universe

Introduction

God has created a fascinating universe! It is full of wonder and beauty. The book of Genesis describes the creation of the world and all things in it (Genesis 1-2). When God finished creation, He said that it was very good. People can get some understanding of the beauty, power, and majesty of God simply by observing His creation. As St. Paul wrote in his letter to the Romans, "For the invisible things of him from the creation of the world are clearly seen, being understood by the things that are made, even his eternal power and Godhead; so that they are without excuse." (Romans 1:20) God's power and divinity can be known by observing the things that He has made, that is, all things in His creation!

In the previous nine books of this Science LIFEPAC® series, you have studied some of the wonders of the earth and the universe that God has made. You have studied plant and animal systems, aspects of chemistry and physics, "spaceship earth," the solar system, and the stars. In this LIFEPAC, you will get an overview of the material covered in the previous nine LIFEPACs of this series. By reviewing the material in this one LIFEPAC, you will hopefully grow in your appreciation and love of God who created all these things in His wisdom and love. In addition, you will discover that God's detailed plan can be seen within all of His Creation, from tiny DNA molecules to the vast galaxies of the universe.

The new vocabulary in this LIFEPAC is limited. Instead, most of the vocabulary to be covered in this LIFEPAC will be reviewed in the vocabulary presented in the previous LIFEPACs. As you go through this LIFEPAC, you may need to refresh your memory of topics and information covered in earlier LIFEPACs. By reviewing this material, your understanding and **retention** of these important science topics should be increased.

Objectives

Read these objectives. These objectives tell what you should be able to do when you have completed this LIFEPAC. When you have completed this LIFEPAC, you should be able to do the following:

1. Describe the plant processes of photosynthesis, transport, and regulation.

2. Describe the digestive, excretory, skeletal, and nervous systems of humans.

3. Discuss genetics and aspects of reproductive systems in plants and animals.

4. Give some examples of biomes and cycles in nature.

5. Explain the nature of matter and relate the various particles to the structure of matter.

6. Explain the main divisions of the Periodic Table of the Elements and identify common chemical symbols.

7. Explain the basic concepts of light and the ways that colors are produced.

8. Explain how sound is produced and describe the characteristics of sound.

9. Explain some basic components of motion such as force, work, laws of motion, and changes in motion.

10. Describe the various motions of earth.

11. Name and describe the various parts of our Solar System.

12. Identify important people, events, and observing equipment in the history of astronomy.

13. Describe how stars differ and identify some of their main characteristics.

Survey the LIFEPAC. Ask yourself some questions about this study and write your questions here.

_____

_____

_____

_____

_____

_____

_____

_____

_____

_____

_____

_____

_____

_____

_____

_____

_____

_____

_____

1. PLANT AND ANIMAL SYSTEMS

Within all plants and animals, there are many complex processes occurring that allow the organism to live, grow, and reproduce. Many parts of plants and animals work together to perform a common function or purpose. We call these complex, interacting parts "systems." When considered carefully, these systems indicate the intelligent design of a loving and wise God.

In this section of the LIFEPAC, you will review some of the complex systems in plants and animals (primarily humans). You will also review information on biomes and cycles in nature. Finally, you will review information on genetics and how various traits are inherited in plants and animals.

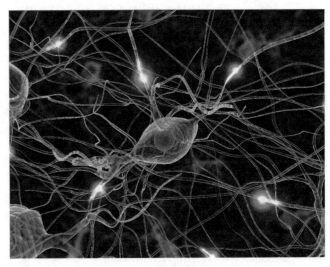

| Plants and animals have complex systems.

Section Objectives

Review these objectives. When you have completed this section, you should be able to:

1. Describe the plant systems of photosynthesis, transport, and regulation.
2. Describe the digestive, excretory, skeletal, and nervous systems of humans.
3. Discuss genetics and aspects of reproductive systems in plants and animals.
4. Give some examples of biomes and cycles in nature.

Vocabulary

Review the vocabulary words in Science LIFEPACS 601, 602, 603, and 604.

Study these words to enhance your learning success in this section.

cytokinins (sī tō kī nənz). A chemical regulator found in coconut milk that causes roots, stems, leaves, and buds to form from one piece of plant tissue.

framework (frām wėrk). A basic structure.

interrelate (in tər ri lāt). To have a mutual relationship.

retention (ri ten shən). The act of retaining, especially the ability to keep things in mind.

Note: *All vocabulary words in this LIFEPAC appear in* **boldface** *print the first time they are used. If you are not sure of the meaning when you are reading, study the definitions given.*

Pronunciation Key: hat, āge, cãre, fär; let, ēqual, tėrm; it, īce; hot, ōpen, ôrder; oil; out; cup, pút, rüle; child; long; thin; /ℱH/ for then; /zh/ for measure; /u/ or /ə/ represents /a/ in about, /e/ in taken, /i/ in pencil, /o/ in lemon, and /u/ in circus.

PLANT SYSTEMS

God created a great variety of plants. Yet, many plants have common systems that help them live, grow, and reproduce. There are three systems common to many plants: the *photo-synthesis* system, the *transport* system, and the *regulatory* system. Let's review the components and processes involved in each one of these plant systems.

Photosynthesis system. *Photosynthesis* is a process in green plants where food is produced with the help of sunlight. The primary location of photosynthesis in green plants is the leaves. That is why we call this location the "leaf factory." Just as industrial factories produce goods in the industrial world, the "leaf factory" takes raw materials and combines them with sunlight to produce food. Green stems in plants can also produce food. In fact, any cell that contains *chlorophyll* can make food.

All factories need a source of energy to produce finished products. This energy could come in the form of electricity, oil and gas, or even water and wind power. The leaf factory also needs a source of energy. Its source of energy is light from the sun. Utilizing the sun's energy, it makes food from water, minerals and other nutrients from the soil, and carbon dioxide, and releases oxygen as a by-product. The oxygen is used by animals for breathing. The "food" produced is initially a sugar called *glucose*. This sugar can be changed into other foods within the plant such as fats, oils, proteins, and vitamins. Some of it gets stored as starch.

As mentioned previously, the primary location of the photosynthesis process within green plants is in the leaf. Within the leaf, photosynthesis takes place primarily in the *palisade* layer. This layer consists of cells lined up like fence posts. These cells are called *chloroplasts* and contain chlorophyll. Cells arranged in this manner get more exposure to sunlight.

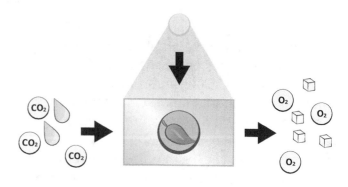

| Photosynthesis process in the leaf factory

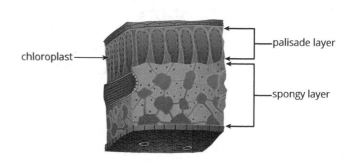

The *spongy* layer in the leaf has some chlorophyll and can make food. It does not make nearly as much food as the palisade layer. The spongy layer has many holes and open spaces which allow gases (carbon dioxide and oxygen) to be exchanged. Generally, water vapor, carbon dioxide, and oxygen are found within the spaces between the cells. Small openings known as *stomata* are located on the underneath side of the leaf. These openings allow gases to enter the spongy layer. The most important function of the spongy layer is the exchange of gases.

The leaf is covered with a protective layer of cells known as the *epidermis*. The cells of the epidermis are covered with a thin waxy layer known as the cuticle. The cuticle is a waxy coat which prevents the loss of water. All of these structures are parts of the *photosynthesis system* within plants.

Complete the following statements.

1.1 The photosynthesis system is located primarily in the _____ .

1.2 The green substance necessary for photosynthesis is called _____ .

1.3 A product made during photosynthesis is a carbohydrate (simple sugar) known as

_____ .

1.4 Sugar is transported to parts of the plant and stored as _____ .

1.5 An important by-product of photosynthesis is _____ .

1.6 The energy for photosynthesis comes from the _____ .

1.7 In addition to glucose and starch, plants can also make other foods such as

a. _____ , b. _____ ,

c. _____ , and d. _____ .

Match these items.

1.8 _____ the waxy protective coating on leaves

1.9 _____ openings that are most frequently found on the underside
of a leaf

1.10 _____ the outer layer of cells of a leaf that has a waxy coating

1.11 _____ the layer within the leaf that has many holes and spaces
for gases to exchange

1.12 _____ the layer in the leaf that is the primary location of
photosynthesis

a. spongy layer

b. palisade layer

c. epidermis

d. stomata

e. cuticle

f. chlorophyll

Transport system. The *transport system* of plants involves three main structures: the roots, the stems, and the leaves. These three structures have a system of tubes which make up the transport system. The tubes that transport water and minerals in this system are known as *xylem*. Tubes that transport food to various parts of the plant are called *phloem*. Together in the stem, the xylem and the phloem are known as a *vascular bundle*. In the root, the xylem and phloem together are known as the *vascular cylinder*. In the leaf, this bundle is called the *vein*. The vascular tissues, regardless of whether they are called the vascular bundle, the vascular cylinder, or the vein, are all composed of xylem and phloem.

Plants must have a continuous supply of water and minerals. Their root hairs take in water and minerals from the soil. These minerals go up the xylem to the stem and leaves. Food is manufactured in the leaves and then transported down the phloem to various parts of the plant. There, it is converted to starch and stored. Storage of foods is an important function of roots. Plants, such as yams, carrots, beets, radishes, and turnips, store food in their roots. Stems and leaves may also act as storage places for food. Storage materials are not limited to starch. Plants may also store fats, oils, vitamins, and proteins.

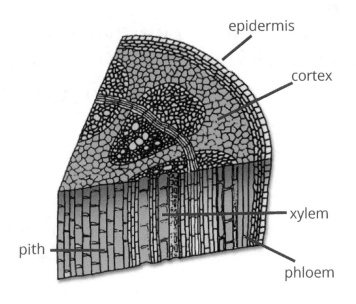

| Stems

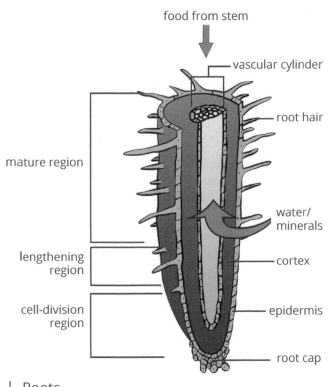

| Roots

Complete the following statements.

1.13 Plants frequently convert glucose into _____ (for storage).

1.14 Plants can also make and store other foods such as a. _____ ,

   b. _____ , c. _____ , and d. _____ .

1.15 The three main structures of the plant which are involved in transport are the

   a. _____ , b. _____ , and the c. _____ .

Match these items.

1.16 _____ the tubes that transport water and minerals   a. vascular cylinder

1.17 _____ the tubes that transport food   b. vascular bundle

1.18 _____ one of the important functions of roots   c. vein

1.19 _____ the name of the xylem and phloem in the stem   d. phloem

1.20 _____ the name of the xylem and phloem in roots   e. xylem

          f. storage of food

Regulatory system. The *regulatory system* of a plant has to do with the processes and chemicals (*regulators*) that help the plant grow. The two types of regulatory chemicals are natural and artificial.

Natural regulators are chemicals normally produced by plants. At just the right time and in just the right place, the plant makes these growth chemicals. For example, when a new root is needed, just the right chemicals are produced to start a new root. When a bud or a flower is needed, just the right chemicals are made by the plant in that spot. *Auxins, gibberellins*, and **cytokinins** are three "families" of these regulator chemicals.

Artificial regulators are chemicals produced by humans. Through their use over the years, it has been found that some artificial chemical regulators are helpful to plant growth and have no harmful side effects, while others help regulate plant growth but have harmful effects to humans or the environment. For example, the regulator *2,4-D* can be used to control weeds and dandelions in other crops and breaks down to form harmless chemicals. But other regulators contain chemicals, such as arsenic and lead, that can have long-term harmful effects in the environment or to humans.

Scientists are exploring and investigating ways to care for and protect the environment. People must use the information learned by scientists to help protect the planet we live on.

Answer true or false.

1.21 _____ The *regulatory system* of a plant has to do with the processes and chemicals (*regulators*) that help the plant grow.

1.22 _____ The two types of regulators for plants are (1) natural and (2) artificial.

1.23 _____ Three "families" of natural regulator chemicals are *auxins*, *gibberellins*, and *cytokinins*.

1.24 _____ Artificial chemical regulators are found naturally in plants.

1.25 _____ Artificial chemical regulators have both helpful and harmful effects.

1.26 _____ We need to use science and the information we learn from it to take better care of the environment we live in.

Complete this activity.

1.27 Write a half-page report on a natural or artificial chemical regulator for plants. You may choose one of those mentioned in this section, or you may write about another regulator that you discover while doing your research. You may find the information contained in Section 3 of the Science 601 LIFEPAC to be helpful. You should also use information that you can find on the Internet, in a library, or from other resources to help you. Be sure to mention the effects that the chemical has on plants and how it is used. Also discuss whether or not the regulator may have any harmful effects.

TEACHER CHECK _____ _____
initials   date

Tropisms. Chemical regulators, especially *auxins*, affect *tropisms* in plants. A *tropism* is the name given to the plant's response that causes it to grow either toward or away from a stimulus. If the plant grows *toward* something, it is a *positive tropism*. If the plant grows *away* from something, it is called a *negative tropism*.

There are three basic types of tropisms: (1) *phototropisms*, (2) *geotropisms*, and (3) *hydrotropisms*.

Plants show positive *photo*tropisms because they turn toward *light*. Plants show both positive and negative *geo*tropisms in relation to the *earth*. The roots show a positive geotropism in growing toward the earth. The leaves show a negative geotropism by growing away from the earth. Finally, *water* causes a *hydro*tropism in plants. The roots of plants show a positive hydrotropism because they grow toward water.

Complete the following statements.

1.28 A plant that grows toward a stimulus has a _____ tropism.

1.29 A plant that grows away from a stimulus has a _____ tropism.

1.30 A hydrotropism is a plant's response to _____ .

1.31 A geotropism is a plant's response to _____ .

1.32 A phototropism is a plant's response to _____ .

ANIMAL AND HUMAN SYSTEMS

Plants are designed in a marvelous way. You have reviewed some of the main "systems" that make up most plants. Animals have been created with various body parts that **interrelate** in a complex fashion. We call these various related parts of animal bodies "body systems." For example, there is a way for animals to eat and digest food in their bodies. We call this the "digestive system." All animals have a digestive system. Human beings have a digestive system, too. In fact, if we examine the various "systems" within the human body, we can get a good idea of the basic operation of most of the "animal systems."

The human body is among the most wonderful parts of nature. The various parts of the human body are very complex and orderly. In this part of the LIFEPAC, we will explore four major "systems" of the human body. They are the digestive system, the excretory system, the skeletal system, and the nervous system. By examining these four systems of the human body in some detail, you will learn about the main body systems common to all animals.

Digestive system. The digestive system acts like a chemical laboratory. It breaks down food into simple chemicals that can be absorbed by other parts of the body. These chemical substances are used as energy sources and building materials for the body. Animals such as worms, insects, mammals, birds, fish, and

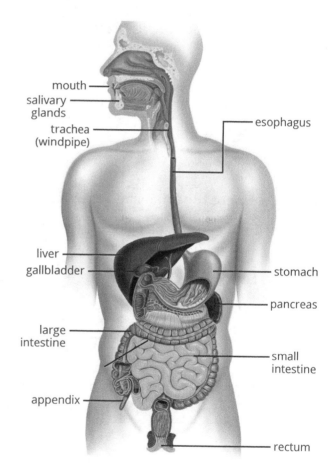

mouth
salivary glands
trachea (windpipe)
esophagus
liver
gallbladder
stomach
pancreas
large intestine
small intestine
appendix
rectum

| The digestive system

people all have digestive systems. Their digestive systems have similar parts and purposes. For the sake of our discussion, we will cover the human digestive system, shown in the illustration. Study this illustration and be sure that you can identify the parts of the digestive system and the pathway of food through the system.

The *alimentary canal* is composed of the parts of the digestive system through which food passes. It consists of the mouth, esophagus, stomach, small intestine, large intestine, and rectum. As food moves through the body, digestive juices are added. This addition of juices helps break down the food into substances that can be absorbed by the body.

Each part of the alimentary canal has a special task to perform. The mouth has two functions. They are to chew and grind the food and to add saliva to help digestion. The esophagus is a tube that allows food to pass from the mouth to the stomach. The stomach churns the food and adds digestive juices. Digestive juices are rich in *enzymes* that help break down the food into chemicals that can be absorbed.

The liver and pancreas are located close to the small intestine. They open into the small intestine and add substances that aid in the breakdown of food. The pancreas adds enzymes. The gallbladder adds *bile* to the process of digestion. Bile turns fats into an *emulsion*. This is very important in the process of breaking fats into smaller particles.

The small intestine functions to absorb food. Finger-like projections on the small intestine are able to absorb food. These finger-like projections are known as *villi*. Villi have an abundance of capillaries, which pick up the nutrients from the food and circulate them to the cells. The large intestine and rectum carry away undigested waste materials from the body. Any excess water is absorbed by the large intestine.

Complete the following activities.

1.33 List these parts of the digestive system or alimentary canal in their proper order: rectum, esophagus, small intestine, mouth, large intestine, and stomach.

a. _____ b. _____ c. _____

d. _____ e. _____ f. _____

1.34 Define the *alimentary canal.* _____

_____

1.35 What are the main functions of the stomach in digesting food? _____

_____

_____

Write the correct letter and answer on each blank.

1.36 The main function of the large intestine is to _____ .

    a. absorb food   b. absorb water

    c. add digestive juices   d. secrete bile

1.37 The main function of the small intestine is to _____ .

    a. absorb food   b. absorb water

    c. add digestive juices   d. secrete bile

1.38 The function of bile is to _____ .
    a. break down sugar   b. digest protein
    c. add enzymes to the stomach   d. make an emulsion of fats

1.39 The pancreas functions in digestion by _____ .
    a. producing bile   b. absorbing fat
    c. producing enzymes   d. helping the liver

1.40 Which one of the following is not part of the alimentary canal? _____
    a. mouth   b. small intestine   c. liver   d. rectum

Excretory system. There are four main parts to the human *excretory system*. They are the blood circulation system, the lungs, the kidneys, and the skin. All of these parts must work together to get rid of the body's waste materials. The *blood circulation system* carries nutrients and oxygen to all of the body's cells. At the same time, it picks up waste materials and carbon dioxide.

In the blood circulation system, the blood takes oxygen from the lungs and carries it to each cell in the body. It also carries nutrients from the villi of the small intestine to feed each body cell. Villi is explained in LIFEPAC 602, Section 1. At the same time, it removes all excess wastes such as water, carbon dioxide, poisons, and urea. The blood disposes of the excess water, urea, poisons, and other liquid wastes through the kidneys. The carbon dioxide gas is removed through the lungs.

Your blood circulation system contains about 12 pints of blood. Your heart beats about 72 times per minute to pump blood through your blood circulation system. Your heart is the finest pump in the world. Nothing that human beings have developed can compare with the reliability of the heart pump.

Arteries are tubes that carry fresh blood away from the heart. They have thick muscular walls that help to force the blood along its path.

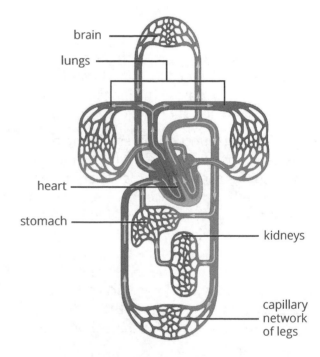

| Blood circulation system

Veins are tubes that carry used blood back to the heart. Veins have thin walls. They also have valves that prevent the blood from flowing backward. Capillaries are very thin tubes, which are only about one cell thick. These tiny tubes unite the arteries and veins. Capillaries make contact with the body's cells. Here, the nutrients and oxygen are supplied to the cells and the wastes removed.

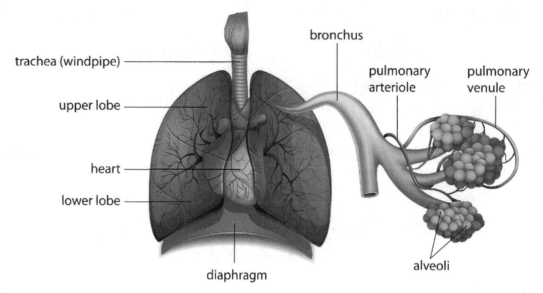

trachea (windpipe)
bronchus
pulmonary arteriole
pulmonary venule
upper lobe
heart
lower lobe
diaphragm
alveoli

| Lungs

The *lungs* are a second part of the excretory system. The major function of the lungs is to purify the blood of gases. The lungs supply oxygen to the blood and get rid of carbon dioxide.

To help the lungs function, air enters the nasal passage and goes down the trachea (windpipe) to the lungs. Air sacs in the lungs are the places where the exchange of gases occurs. Capillaries line the air sacs to bring the red blood cells to this area. The red blood cells pick up oxygen in the air sacs and carry it to the body's cells. The oxygen is carried on *hemoglobin*, an iron-rich protein that makes up a large part of the red blood cells. Oxygen attaches to the hemoglobin and circulates with the blood to the body's cells.

A third part of the excretory system is the *kidneys*. The kidneys purify the liquid part of the blood. Thousands of filters in each kidney purify the blood. All of the blood passes through this purification system. The kidneys remove poisons, salts, water, urea, and other waste materials. Waste material removed from the blood is called urine. The bladder serves as a storage area for this waste urine. It is necessary to drink plenty of water for this filtering system to work properly and to carry off the wastes.

The fourth and final part of the excretory system is the *skin*. The skin helps us to get rid of waste through perspiration. It also functions as a protective coating and cooling system for the body. Evaporation of moisture helps to cool the body. The skin prevents germs and dirt from entering our bodies. It must be kept clean if it is to function properly. Oil and sweat will clog the pores of the skin and cause skin disorders. Also, the skin is important to keep us in contact with our environment by sensing stimuli, such as hot or cold. Throughout the skin, tiny nerve endings perform this function.

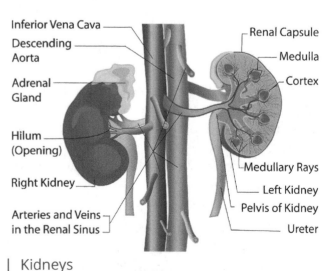

Inferior Vena Cava
Descending Aorta
Adrenal Gland
Hilum (Opening)
Right Kidney
Arteries and Veins in the Renal Sinus
Renal Capsule
Medulla
Cortex
Medullary Rays
Left Kidney
Pelvis of Kidney
Ureter

| Kidneys

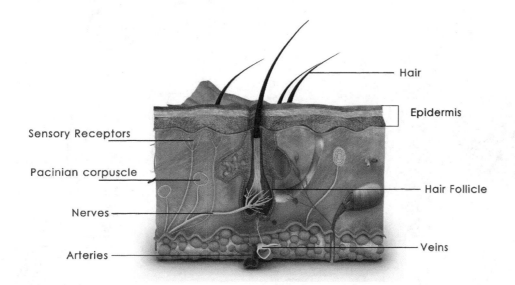

| Skin

  Complete the following statements.

1.41 The first line of protection, which prevents germs and dirt from entering the body, is the

_____ .

1.42 The major waste product eliminated by the lungs is _____ .

1.43 Hemoglobin is an iron-rich protein that carries _____ to the cells.

1.44 Urea is one of the major waste products that is removed by the _____ .

1.45 The blood picks up nutrients from the _____ of the small intestine.

1.46 The organ that serves as a cooling system for the body by means of evaporation is the

_____ .

1.47 The major difference between arteries and veins is the thick muscular walls in the

a. _____ and valves in the b. _____ .

1.48 Tiny tubes that unite arteries and veins are known as _____ .

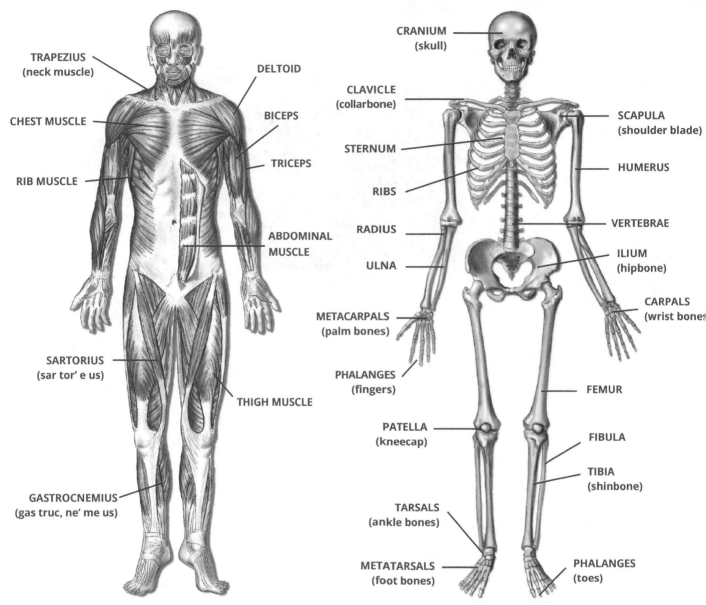

| Skeletal muscles

| Major bones of the skeleton

Skeletal system. Another major system of the human body is the *skeletal system*. The skeletal system is composed of the *muscles* and *bones*. This system gives form to the body and allows movement. The body has 206 bones. These bones provide support like a **framework**. Some bones are hollow. These bones are unusually strong. They carry the body weight. Leg bones are examples of very strong, hollow bones. Bones carry out another important function. Red blood cells and some white cells are made in the region inside the bone called the *marrow*.

Marrow is the spongy inner portion of certain bones. The major bones of the body are shown in the illustration "Major bones of the body skeleton." Take some time now to review these bones and their locations.

Muscles fit over the body's skeleton. They allow movement and motion of the body. Some of the major muscles of the body are shown in the illustration "Skeletal muscles." Take some time now to review these muscles and their locations.

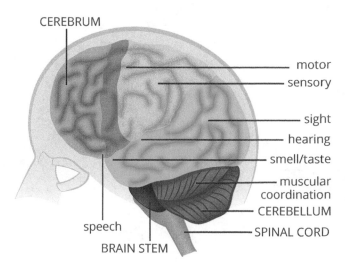

CEREBRUM

motor
sensory
sight
hearing
smell/taste
muscular
coordination
CEREBELLUM
SPINAL CORD

speech
BRAIN STEM

| Parts of the brain

Muscles are voluntary or involuntary. Both voluntary and involuntary muscles are operated from the brain. You can control some parts of your body by thinking about them and moving them. The involuntary actions of your body are operated by the medulla, which is part of the brain stem. They control necessary life processes such as digestion, circulation, breathing, and heartbeat. These processes continue even while we are asleep.

Nervous system. The *nervous system* enables people and animals to respond to their environment. The *central nervous system* consists of the brain, the spinal cord, and nerves. Our human brain is different from those of animals. We are capable of abstract thoughts, reasoning, creative thinking, and logical solution of problems. We are also able to project our thoughts into the future and to use symbols.

The human brain has three main sections: (1) the cerebrum, (2) the cerebellum, and (3) the brain stem. These sections control various functions. The cerebrum is the location of intelligence and thought. It gives us the ability to learn, reason, remember, create, and think.

It also controls the senses and the muscles. The cerebellum coordinates all the muscles so that they work together. The brain stem, is a stalk-like structure that connects the brain with the spinal cord. It has several different parts that control various functions in the body. Among these functions controlled by the brain stem are breathing, heartbeat, and reflexes such as sneezing, blinking of the eyes, and swallowing. Body temperature, hunger, and other internal conditions of the body are controlled by the parts of the brain stem.

From the brain stem, twelve pairs of nerve bundles move down the spinal cord to the rest of the body. These nerves are connected to the sense organs, muscles, facial glands, and vital organs. They are like many tiny strands of wire bundled together and wrapped with a cover. The twelve pairs of nerve bundles branch out as they come up the spinal cord to the brain stem into thirty-one pairs of special nerve bundles that connect every part of the brain.

The nervous system is like a large broadcasting system that transmits messages throughout the body. The *neuron*, or nerve cell, acts to transmit these electrical signals. A nerve cell has three basic parts. They are the *axon*, the *dendrite*, and the *synapse*. The axon is the transmitting end of the neuron. The dendrite is the receiving end. The dendrites of one neuron do not quite touch the axons of other neurons, but they are very close. The synapse is the small space between the dendrites and axons where the nerve impulses are electrically transmitted.

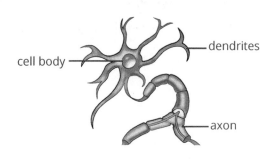

cell body
dendrites
axon

| The nerve cell or neuron

Place the correct letter on each blank.

1.49 The clavicle is the _____ .

a. arm   b. skull   c. leg   d. collar bone

1.50 The cranium is a bone of the _____ .

a. arm   b. skull   c. leg   d. chest

1.51 The carpals are bones which make up the _____ .

a. fingers and toes   b. wrist   c. knee   d. ankle

1.52 The patella is a bone of the _____ .

a. knee   b. ankle   c. hip   d. neck

1.53 The phalanges are bones which make up the _____ .

a. fingers and toes   b. wrist   c. spine   d. vertebrae

1.54 The gastrocnemius is a muscle located in the _____ .

a. arm   b. chest   c. leg   d. neck

1.55 The biceps and triceps are muscles of the _____ .

a. leg   b. arm   c. neck   d. stomach

1.56 The trapezius muscle is located in the _____ .

a. leg   b. arm   c. stomach   d. neck

Match these items.

1.57 _____ the part of the brain that controls breathing, heartbeat, and reflexes such as sneezing, blinking, and swallowing

1.58 _____ the location of intelligence and thought

1.59 _____ the transmitting end of a neuron

1.60 _____ the receiving end of a neuron

1.61 _____ the small space between neurons where nerve impulses are passed from one neuron to another

1.62 _____ the area of the brain that controls muscle coordination

a. synapse

b. dendrite

c. axon

d. cerebrum

e. cerebellum

f. brain stem

g. neuron

GENETICS AND REPRODUCTION

One of the most striking things about people, animals, and plants is the fact that each reproduces its own kind. Each inherits traits from its parents. This transfer of traits is due to a special molecule in cells known as the *DNA molecule*. A study of this molecule and how it dictates traits in cells is known as *molecular genetics*.

Gregor Mendel discovered the principle of *dominance* in his work with garden peas. Certain traits like color, size, shape, and texture influence other traits. Carl Correns used four-o'clocks to demonstrate a blending of traits called *incomplete dominance*.

Genes carry a message for each trait in molecules of DNA. One of the main parts of the DNA molecule is sugar-phosphate. A change in a gene that produces a new, inheritable trait is called a *mutation*.

R. C. Punnett suggested a system of squares that helps organize genetic data. Punnett Squares are used to predict the characteristics of offspring. A cross between a male hybrid black guinea pig (Bb) and a female hybrid black guinea pig (Bb) produces young with the following genetic make-up:

Cells reproduce themselves by splitting apart. This kind of cell division is called mitosis. They have the same number of chromosomes as the parent cell. Mitosis is the type of cell division that occurs both as organisms grow larger and when worn-out cells are replaced.

	B	b	
B	BB	Bb	25% purebred black
			50% hybrid black
b	Bb	bb	25% purebred white

Most multicellular plants and animals reproduce themselves by a process called *sexual reproduction*. Cells called sperm and egg are part of sexual reproduction. The sperm cell from a male parent and an egg from a female parent join together. This process begins a new life. For example, in plants, the sperm in pollen unites with the egg in the plant ovule. Before pollen and egg unite, the cells must undergo a special kind of division known as *reduction division*. Reduction division is a type of cell division in which chromosomes are reduced. In a plant that has fourteen chromosomes, the chromosomes in the pollen will be reduced to seven and the chromosomes in the egg will be reduced to seven. When the pollen and egg unite, the chromosomes unite and the plant embryo that is formed will have fourteen chromosomes. Also, the plant that develops will have the constant number of chromosomes, which is fourteen in this example.

Reduction division assures that the plant will be restored to the constant number of chromosomes. It will receive traits from both parents. This method of reduction occurs only in reproductive cells. All other cells reproduce by mitosis. These methods of cell reproduction give a plant or animal a constant number of chromosomes.

Complete this reading assignment.

Locate your Science 604 LIFEPAC on Molecular Genetics. Carefully review and study the topics listed below, found in Sections 2 and 3 of the Science 604 LIFEPAC, and place a check mark in the box when you have completed each step. You may want to obtain additional information on these topics from the Internet, library, or other resources if you need to better understand these topics.

☐ 1.   Be sure you can summarize Gregor Mendel's work with tall and dwarf garden peas.

☐ 2.   Review the system of genetic symbols and the method of setting up a Punnett Square.

☐ 3.   Carefully study the meaning of *incomplete dominance*.

☐ 4.   Study the role of the DNA molecule in transmitting traits.

☐ 5.   Be sure you can define a *mutation*.

☐ 6.   Learn the major parts of the DNA molecule:

   (a) the deoxyribose sugar,

   (b) the phosphate,

   (c) the spiral shape, and

   (d) the importance of the base pairs in forming the alphabet to spell out traits.

Complete this activity when you have finished the above reading assignment.

1.63   Solve this problem. Mendel discovered that the purple-colored pea flowers dominated recessive white ones. Let the large P represent purple and small p represent white flowers. Assume that a hybrid plant with Pp (dominant purple and recessive white) is self-pollinated.

What fraction of the new flowers would be white (recessive pp)? _____

If you have difficulty solving this problem, review the appropriate parts of Section 2 in the Science 604 LIFEPAC. The problem is set up and solved like the sample problem of Mendel's tall and dwarf peas. Remember, you are crossing Pp with Pp just as the sample problem was Tt and Tt.

Match these items.

1.64 _____ cell division in which new cells have the same number of chromosomes as the parent cell

1.65 _____ cell division in which the new cells have one-half of the original number of chromosomes

1.66 _____ a condition in which neither gene of a pair is dominant; instead, they show a blended effect

1.67 _____ a change in a gene that forms a new trait that can be inherited

1.68 _____ the person who devised a system of squares used to record genetic problems

1.69 _____ the person who discovered the principle of dominance

1.70 _____ the person who experimented with four-o'clocks

1.71 _____ the special molecule that is able to store and recover information about traits

1.72 _____ one of the main parts of the DNA molecule

a. sugar-phosphate

b. Carl Correns

c. mutation

d. mitosis

e. Gregor Mendel

f. DNA

g. traits

h. incomplete dominance

i. R. C. Punnett

j. reduction division

ECOLOGICAL SYSTEMS

An *ecological system* involves the plants, animals, people, environment, and all the interactions that occur between them in a given area of the earth. Ecological systems are often subdivided into groupings called *biomes*. A biome may be defined as a major ecological grouping of plants and animals. Each biome has its own special groups of plants and animals. In this portion of the LIFEPAC, you will review six of the major terrestrial biomes. *Terrestrial biomes* are groups that occur on earth (land). Those which occur in water are called *aquatic biomes*.

The kinds of plants and animals found within a biome are largely determined by the climate. For example, a *tropical rain forest* with all of its inhabitants is quite different from a forest of hardwoods in the mountainous temperate zone. Furthermore, these also are different from a *tundra biome*. The kinds of life found in a tundra biome are different because of the harsh climate. The tundra is treeless. Plants found there are mostly lichens, mosses, and a few that bear flowers. Animal life of the tundra includes the polar bear, caribou, snowshoe hare, and some birds.

The *northern coniferous forest* comprises the northernmost forests of conifers. It contains moose, black bears, wolves, rodents, and birds. The *deciduous forests* contain trees that shed their leaves. *Grasslands* are the plains and prairies. *Deserts* are dry and are characterized by specialized plants, principally types of cacti.

In contrast, a *tropical rain forest* has a hot and humid climate. Plant life there is abundant. Many species of animals are found in a tropical rain forest. The lush vegetation in such a forest can support many kinds of animals.

 Read and review the part on "Terrestrial biomes" in Section 3 of the Science 603 LIFEPAC. As you read it, complete the following activity.

 Complete this activity.

1.73 Write a brief description of each of these terrestrial biomes.

a. tundra _____

_____

_____

_____

_____

_____

b. northern coniferous forest _____

_____

_____

_____

_____

c. deciduous forest _____

_____

_____

_____

_____

d. grassland _____

_____

_____

_____

_____

e. tropical rain forest _____

_____

_____

_____

_____

f. desert _____

_____

_____

_____

_____

Aquatic biomes are those that occur in bodies of water. A biome in salty ocean water has different plants and animals than that of a freshwater pond. Even the different depths of the ocean have different groups of plants and animals.

One of the major characteristics of aquatic biomes is the presence of a food chain. A typical food chain from an ocean biome might read this way:

algae › protozoa, tiny crustaceans › small fish › larger fish

Another characteristic common to all biomes, both terrestrial and aquatic, is the presence of *cycles*. Within any biome is a constant turnover, or circulation, of substances. This turnover is referred to as a *cycle*. Cycles of minerals, carbon, water, nitrogen, and many other substances are common. Two cycles that are characteristic of every biome are the *nitrogen cycle* and the *carbon-oxygen-hydrogen cycle* (also called the *carbon cycle*).

In the nitrogen cycle, legumes like alfalfa, soybeans, and peas take and hold atmospheric nitrogen so that it can be used by plants. When plants die, bacteria and fungi release the nitrogen compounds back into the atmosphere.

In the carbon-oxygen-hydrogen cycle, animals consume oxygen and release carbon dioxide and water. During decay, the same products are given off. Plants take up the carbon dioxide and water, produce carbohydrates for food, and give off oxygen.

 Review. It will be helpful to review the part of "Cycles" in Section 3 of the Science 603 LIFEPAC.

 Complete the following activities.

1.74 What plants are capable of fixing atmospheric nitrogen into a form that can be used by plants?

_____

_____

1.75 What organisms are able to degrade the decaying material to allow nitrogen to be returned to the atmosphere? _____

1.76 What group of organisms produce oxygen for the carbon cycle? _____

1.77 What group of organisms produce carbohydrates for the carbon cycle? _____

TEACHER CHECK _____ _____

initials   date

 Review the material in this section in preparation for the Self Test. The Self Test will check your mastery of this particular section. The items missed on this Self Test will indicate specific areas where restudy is needed for mastery.

SELF TEST 1

Match these items (each answer, 2 points).

1.01	_____ the location of most photosynthesis	a. hemoglobin
1.02	_____ a by-product of photosynthesis	b. urine
1.03	_____ openings found on the underside of a leaf	c. mutation
1.04	_____ a common storage product of plants	d. absorbs food
1.05	_____ the first stable product made during photosynthesis	e. absorbs water
1.06	_____ the name of the tubes that transport food in plants	f. geotropism
1.07	_____ the name of the tubes that transport water and minerals in plants	g. xylem
		h. phloem
1.08	_____ the name of the vascular bundle in the leaf	i. starch
1.09	_____ a natural plant regulator	j. glucose
1.010	_____ a response to gravity	k. stomata
1.011	_____ the main function of the large intestine	l. leaf
1.012	_____ the main function of the small intestine	m. oxygen
1.013	_____ an iron-rich protein that carries oxygen to the cells	n. vein
1.014	_____ a liquid waste product eliminated from the blood	o. vascular cylinder
1.015	_____ a change in a gene that forms a new trait that can be inherited	p. auxin
		q. carbon dioxide

Answer true or false (each answer, 1 point).

1.016 _____ Bacteria on legumes are able to release nitrogen into the air.

1.017 _____ Carl Correns devised the Punnett Square.

1.018 _____ Mitosis results in new cells with the same number of chromosomes as the parent cell from which they came.

1.019 _____ The tundra biome does not have trees.

1.020 _____ Bile breaks down proteins for digestion.

1.021 _____ A characteristic common to all biomes is the presence of cycles such as the nitrogen cycle.

1.022 _____ The DNA molecule has a sugar-phosphate structure.

1.023 _____ The cerebellum is the location of intelligence and thought.

1.024 _____ The brain stem controls breathing and heartbeat.

1.025 _____ A dendrite is the "sending end" of a neuron.

1.026 _____ The cerebrum controls the coordination of muscles.

1.027 _____ The bone marrow makes red blood cells.

1.028 _____ The skin acts as a cooling system by means of evaporation.

1.029 _____ Digestive juices are rich in enzymes.

1.030 _____ Gibberellin is an artificial plant regulator made by man.

Complete the following statements (each answer, 3 points).

1.031 The patella is a bone located in the _____ .

1.032 The energy for photosynthesis comes from the _____ .

1.033 Food tubes that make up the transport system of plants are called _____ .

1.034 Phototropism is a response to _____ .

1.035 Hydrotropism is a response to _____ .

1.036 The gallbladder secretes a substance known as _____ , which emulsifies fat.

1.037 Arteries are tubes that carry blood _____ (direction) the heart.

1.038 The kidneys purify the liquid part of the _____ .

1.039 The collar bone is known as the _____ .

1.040 The gastrocnemius muscle is located in the _____ region.

1.041 The cranium is a bone located in the _____ .

1.042 The name given to the nerve cell is a _____ .

1.043 The area between the axon and dendrite that carries nerve impulses is known as the _____ .

1.044 The person who discovered the principle of dominance was _____ .

1.045 The special molecule which is able to store and recover information about genetic traits is _____ .

Complete the following activities (each answer, 5 points).

1.046 Distinguish between voluntary and involuntary muscles.

_____

_____

_____

_____

_____

1.047 Describe how plants, animals, and humans benefit each other in the carbon-oxygen-hydrogen cycle.

_____

_____

_____

_____

_____

SCORE _____   TEACHER _____ _____
                                          initials   date

2. CHEMISTRY AND PHYSICS

In this section of the LIFEPAC, you will review topics related to chemistry and **physics**. Science attempts to study the structure and principles of the universe and make them understandable to man. This is particularly true of the sciences of chemistry and physics. *Chemistry* is the science that deals with the structure and composition of matter and the changes that it undergoes. *Physics* is the science that deals with matter, energy, and the physical properties of different materials. The study of light, sound, and motion are also subjects **pertaining** to the science of physics. You will review materials on all these subjects in this section of the LIFEPAC.

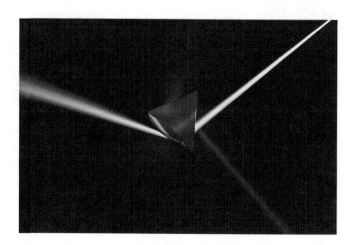

Section Objectives

Review this objective. When you have completed this section, you should be able to:

5. Explain the nature of matter and relate the various particles to the structure of matter.

6. Explain the main divisions of the Periodic Table of the Elements and identify common chemical symbols.

7. Explain the basic concepts of light and the ways that colors are produced.

8. Explain how sound is produced and describe the characteristics of sound.

9. Explain some basic components of motion such as force, work, laws of motion, and changes in motion.

Vocabulary

Review the vocabulary words in Science LIFEPACS 605, 606, and 607.

Study these words to enhance your learning success in this section.

pertaining (pər tān ing). To belong to something as part of it.

physics (fiz iks). The science that deals with matter and energy and their interactions.

Pronunciation Key: hat, āge, cãre, fär; let, ēqual, tėrm; it, īce; hot, ōpen, ôrder; oil; out; cup, pùt, rüle; child; long; thin; /ŦH/ for then; /zh/ for measure; /u/ or /ə/ represents /a/ in about, /e/ in taken, /i/ in pencil, /o/ in lemon, and /u/ in circus.

SCIENCE 610

LIFEPAC TEST

NAME _____

DATE _____

SCORE _____

SCIENCE 610: LIFEPAC TEST

Match these items (each answer, 2 points).

1.	_____	the loudness of sound
2.	_____	a growth chemical made by plants
3.	_____	xylem and phloem bundles in the leaf
4.	_____	the color produced by mixing green and red light
5.	_____	a by-product of photosynthesis
6.	_____	a substance whose molecules consist of atoms that are chemically united
7.	_____	openings found on the underside of a leaf
8.	_____	iron-rich protein that carries oxygen
9.	_____	the person who experimented with incomplete dominance in four-o'clocks
10.	_____	the person who discovered radio waves from space
11.	_____	the person who discovered the principle of dominance
12.	_____	organisms that fix nitrogen on the roots of legumes
13.	_____	liquid waste eliminated from the blood
14.	_____	the rate of doing work
15.	_____	a major division of the Periodic Table
16.	_____	the curving pathway in space
17.	_____	the shape of the earth's orbit around the sun
18.	_____	developed refracting telescope for astronomy

a. Gregor Mendel
b. hemoglobin
c. Galileo
d. ellipse
e. orbit
f. oxygen
g. compound
h. Carl Correns
i. veins
j. stomata
k. auxin
l. yellow
m. Karl Jansky
n. bacteria
o. urine
p. nonmetals
q. power
r. orange
s. amplitude

PERIODIC TABLE OF THE ELEMENTS

NAME _____

PERIODIC TABLE OF THE ELEMENTS

Metals

	1	2	3	4	5	6	7	8	9

Alkali Metals · Alkaline Earth Metals · Transition Metals · Lanthanides · Actinides · Metalloids

Period 1

1	1
H	
Hydrogen	
1.00794	

Period 2

3	2,1	4	2,2
Li		**Be**	
Lithium		Beryllium	
6.941		9.012082	

Period 3

11	2,8,1	12	2,8,2
Na		**Mg**	
Sodium		Magnesium	
22.989770		24.3050	

Period 4

19	2,8,8,1	20	2,8,8,2	21	2,8,9,2	22	2,8,10,2	23	2,8,11,2	24	2,8,13,1	25	2,8,13,2	26	2,8,14,2	27
K		**Ca**		**Sc**		**Ti**		**V**		**Cr**		**Mn**		**Fe**		**Co**
Potassium		Calcium		Scandium		Titanium		Vanadium		Chromium		Manganese		Iron		Cobalt
39.0983		40.078		44.955910		47.867		50.9415		51.9961		54.938049		55.845		58.933200

Period 5

37	2,8,18,8,1	38	2,8,18,8,2	39	2,8,18,9,2	40	2,8,18,10,2	41	2,8,18,12,1	42	2,8,18,13,1	43	2,8,18,13,2	44	2,8,18,15,1	45
Rb		**Sr**		**Y**		**Zr**		**Nb**		**Mo**		**Tc**		**Ru**		**Rh**
Rubidium		Strontium		Yttrium		Zirconium		Niobium		Molybdenum		Technetium		Ruthenium		Rhodium
85.4678		87.62		88.90585		91.224		92.90638		95.94		98		101.07		102.9055

Period 6

55	2,8,18,18,8,1	56	2,8,18,18,8,2	57–71	72	2,8,18,32,10,2	73	2,8,18,32,11,2	74	2,8,18,32,12,2	75	2,8,18,32,13,2	76	2,8,18,32,14,2	77
Cs		**Ba**			**Hf**		**Ta**		**W**		**Re**		**Os**		**Ir**
Cesium		Barium			Hafnium		Tantalum		Tungsten		Rhenium		Osmium		Iridium
132.90545		137.327			178.49		180.9479		183.84		186.207		190.23		192.217

Period 7

87	2,8,18,32,18,8,1	88	2,8,18,32,18,8,2	89–103	104	2,8,18,32,32,10,2	105	2,8,18,32,32,11,2	106	2,8,18,32,32,12,2	107	2,8,18,32,32,13,2	108	2,8,18,32,32,14,2	109
Fr		**Ra**			**Rf**		**Db**		**Sg**		**Bh**		**Hs**		**Mt**
Francium		Radium			Rutherfordium		Dubnium		Seaborgium		Bohrium		Hassium		Meitnerium
(223)		(226)			261		262		266		264		269		268

PERIOD	SHELL	MAXIMUM ELECTRONS IN SHELL
1	K	2
2	L	8
3	M	18
4	N	32
5	O	50
6	P	72

Lanthanides

57	2,8,18,18,9,2	58	2,8,18,19,9,2	59	2,8,18,21,8,2	60	2,8,18,22,8,2	61	2,8,18,23,8,2	62
La		**Ce**		**Pr**		**Nd**		**Pm**		**Sm**
Lanthanum		Cerium		Praseodymium		Neodymium		Promethium		Samarium
138.9055		140.116		140.90765		144.24		145		150.36

Actinides

89	2,8,18,32,18,9,2	90	2,8,18,32,18,10,2	91	2,8,18,32,20,9,2	92	2,8,18,32,21,9,2	93	2,8,18,32,22,9,2	94
Ac		**Th**		**Pa**		**U**		**Np**		**Pu**
Actinium		Thorium		Protactinium		Uranium		Neptunium		Plutonium
227		232.0381		231.03588		238.02891		237		244

Tt Radioactive Element

| 10 | 11 | 12 | 13 | 14 | 15 | 16 | 17 | 18 |

Nonmetals

Other Nonmetals

Halogens

Noble Gases

								2 He Helium 4.002602 2
			5 B Boron 10.811 2 3	6 C Carbon 12.0107 2 4	7 N Nitrogen 14.0067 2 5	8 O Oxygen 15.9994 2 6	9 F Fluorine 18.9984032 2 7	10 Ne Neon 20.1797 2 8
			13 Al Aluminum 26.981538 2 8 3	14 Si Silicon 28.0855 2 8 4	15 P Phosphorus 30.973761 2 8 5	16 S Sulfur 32.065 2 8 6	17 Cl Chlorine 35.453 2 8 7	18 Ar Argon 39.948 2 8 8
Ni Nickel 58.6934 2 8 16 2	29 Cu Copper 63.546 2 8 18 1	30 Zn Zinc 65.39 2 8 18 2	31 Ga Gallium 69.723 2 8 18 3	32 Ge Germanium 72.64 2 8 18 4	33 As Arsenic 74.92160 2 8 18 5	34 Se Selenium 78.96 2 8 18 6	35 Br Bromine 79.904 2 8 18 7	36 Kr Krypton 83.798 2 8 18 8
Pd Palladium 106.42 2 8 18 18 0	47 Ag Silver 107.8682 2 8 18 18 1	48 Cd Cadmium 112.411 2 8 18 18 2	49 In Indium 114.818 2 8 18 18 3	50 Sn Tin 118.710 2 8 18 18 4	51 Sb Antimony 121.760 2 8 18 18 5	52 Te Tellurium 127.60 2 8 18 18 6	53 I Iodine 126.90447 2 8 18 18 7	54 Xe Xenon 131.293 2 8 18 18 8
Pt Platinum 195.078 2 8 18 32 17 1	79 Au Gold 196.96655 2 8 18 32 18 1	80 Hg Mercury 200.59 2 8 18 32 18 2	81 Tl Thallium 204.3833 2 8 18 32 18 3	82 Pb Lead 207.2 2 8 18 32 18 4	83 Bi Bismuth 208.98038 2 8 18 32 18 5	84 Po Polonium 289 2 8 18 32 18 6	85 At Astatine 210 2 8 18 32 18 7	86 Rn Radon (222) 2 8 18 32 18 8
Ds nstadtium 271 2 8 18 32 32 17	111 ○Rg Roentgenium 272 2 8 18 32 32 18 1	112 ○Cn Copernicium 285 2 8 18 32 32 18 2	113 ○Uut Ununtrium 284 2 8 18 32 32 18 3	114 ○Fl Flerovium 289 2 8 18 32 32 18 4	115 ○Uup Ununpentium 288 2 8 18 32 32 18 5	116 ○Lv Livermorium 292 2 8 18 32 32 18 6	117 ○Uus Ununseptium 294 2 8 18 32 32 18	118 ○Uuo Ununoctium 294 2 8 18 32 32 18 8

| Eu uropium 151.964 2 8 18 25 8 2 | 64 ○Gd Gadolinium 157.25 2 8 18 25 9 2 | 65 ○Tb Terbium 158.92534 2 8 18 27 8 2 | 66 ○Dy Dysprosium 162.500 2 8 18 28 8 2 | 67 ○Ho Holmium 164.93032 2 8 18 29 8 2 | 68 ○Er Erbium 167.259 2 8 18 30 8 2 | 69 ○Tm Thulium 168.93421 2 8 18 31 8 2 | 70 ○Yb Ytterbium 173.04 2 8 18 32 8 2 | 71 ○Lu Lutetium 174.967 2 8 18 32 9 2 |
| Am mericium 243 2 8 18 32 25 8 2 | 96 Cm Curium 247 2 8 18 32 25 9 2 | 97 Bk Berkelium 247 2 8 18 32 27 8 2 | 98 Cf Californium 251 2 8 18 32 28 8 2 | 99 ○Es Einsteinium 252 2 8 18 32 29 8 2 | 100 ○Fm Fermium 257 2 8 18 32 30 8 2 | 101 ○Md Mendelevium 258 2 8 18 32 31 8 2 | 102 ○No Nobelium 259 2 8 18 32 32 8 2 | 103 ○Lr Lawrencium 262 2 8 18 32 32 9 2 |

 ○ Man-made Element ○ Rare Earth Element

Answer true or false (each answer, 1 point).

19. _____ Isaac Newton invented the reflecting telescope.

20. _____ The palisade layer of the leaf is the main place where photosynthesis occurs.

21. _____ 2,4-D is a natural plant regulator.

22. _____ The main function of bile is to digest protein.

23. _____ A tropical rain forest biome has lush vegetation with many animals.

24. _____ Mutations are changes in the gene that can be inherited.

25. _____ Light travels slower in glass than in air.

26. _____ Sound travels faster in air than in steel.

27. _____ When 5 pounds are moved 7 feet, 12 foot-pounds of work is done.

28. _____ Inertia keeps the earth moving in its orbit.

29. _____ The sun is yellow in color.

Identify the symbols (each answer, 1 point).

30. Write the chemical name after each symbol.

   a. K _____   b. Na _____   c. N _____

   d. O _____   e. C _____   f. H _____

Complete these statements (each completed statement, 3 points).

31. Three ways stars differ are a. _____ , b. _____ , and c. _____ .

32. Fraunhofer lines help to identify _____ .

33. The sun is the brightest star because _____ .

34. The cerebellum is the center of all _____ .

35. The cerebrum is the location of _____ .

36. Bone marrow manufactures _____ .

37. The small space between the axon and dendrite of a neuron is the _____ .

38 The chromosphere is _____

   _____ .

39. The longest day of the year in the Northern Hemisphere is about _____ .

Complete the following activities (each numbered item, 5 points).

40. Briefly tell the difference between a lunar and solar eclipse.

_____

_____

_____

_____

_____

41. Briefly tell the main functions of the skin.

_____

_____

_____

_____

_____

42. Briefly describe a desert biome.

_____

_____

_____

_____

_____

43. Briefly describe some modern developments in astronomy, beginning in the 1950s.

_____

_____

_____

_____

_____

MATTER

Everything in the world is composed of matter. Matter is anything that occupies space and has mass. Mass refers to the amount of matter in a body. Mass may be considered equal to weight on planet Earth. Weight is a measure of the amount of pull exerted by gravity. An object may be weightless in space, but it will still contain the same amount of mass.

States of matter. Matter in the universe is found in three different states: solid, liquid, and gas. A gas has no shape of its own; it takes the shape of its container. A gas can be allowed to expand into a larger container or it can be compressed or squeezed into a smaller container. It has no fixed volume.

A liquid has no specific shape. It takes on the shape of its container. A liquid has a fixed volume. A liquid cannot be either compressed or squeezed (except for such a tiny amount that its volume is considered the same as fixed).

A solid has a specific shape and a fixed volume. A piece of steel is an example of a solid. Its shape and volume remain the same; although, its shape can be changed into shapes by man.

Elements and atoms. An element is a pure substance that cannot be broken down by chemical means. For example, pure silver is an element. Pure silver cannot be broken down by chemical means into a simpler substance. The very smallest particle of pure silver would be an atom. The smallest part of any pure element is an atom. An atom is so small it cannot be seen. The presence of atoms can be determined by the way they chemically react. They also may be identified by X-ray.

Molecules. A molecule may be made of two or more atoms, or even thousands of atoms. Simple salts and acids sometimes consist of two or three different kinds of atoms. Substances within the human body are so complex they may consist of thousands of atoms. A molecule is defined as the chemical combination of two

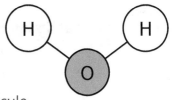

| Water molecule

or more atoms. If the atoms that are combined are different from each other, the result is a compound.

Compounds. When atoms of one kind combine with atoms of another kind, compounds are formed. For example, when two atoms of hydrogen unite with one atom of oxygen, water is formed. Water is written H_2O. It is a compound of hydrogen and oxygen. This compound always has molecules made of hydrogen and oxygen in exactly the same proportion. A compound may be defined as a substance whose molecules consist of atoms that are chemically united.

Examples of some common compounds are sodium chloride (table salt) written as NaCl. Sodium chloride is one atom of sodium and one chlorine atom. Carbon dioxide is CO_2. Carbon dioxide is a compound whose molecules consist of one atom of carbon and two atoms of oxygen. The two represents the number of oxygen atoms in this compound. You will recall that the number one is not written when you have one atom of each element in a compound. The one is understood.

A compound may bear no resemblance to the elements that composed it. For example, sodium is a metal and chlorine is a gas. Both are poisonous. When these two elements combine, the compound formed is table salt. When hydrogen unites with oxygen, water is formed.

Chemical symbols. Chemists use symbols to stand for elements. Symbols are like abbreviations. Each symbol consists of a single capital letter or a capital and a lowercase letter. Some of the symbols are taken from the Latin names for the elements. Chemical symbols are used in chemical formulas.

Complete this assignment.

Refer to the Periodic Table. Study the names and symbols of the elements listed in the table. To do this, try placing a strip of paper over the name of the element and learn its symbol. Then, place the strip of paper over the symbol and make sure you know its proper name. On a separate piece of paper, practice writing the symbol for each element. Then write the name for each symbol.

TEACHER CHECK _____ _____
                                          initials   date

The Periodic Table. The Periodic Table lists the elements in the order of their atomic numbers. The atomic number is the number of protons in the nucleus. Just below the atomic number is the symbol for that element. Below the symbol is the atomic weight of that element. You will recall that atomic weights are not actual weights. They are weights compared to the carbon atom which weighs 12. For example, magnesium weighs twice as much as carbon. Therefore, magnesium weighs (2 x 12) or twenty-four. The weight of all atoms is compared to carbon. This system of comparing atomic weights is known as *relative weight*.

Assignment. Within Section 3 of LIFEPAC 605, study the subsection entitled DIAGRAMS OF ATOMS. Practice making a diagram of the helium and carbon atoms. Use a separate sheet of paper for your diagram. Study the Periodic Table. Check the box as you locate each of the following things from that table.

☐ 1.   The metals.

☐ 2.   The nonmetals.

☐ 3.   A period (a period runs across the chart).

☐ 4.   The rare earth elements.

☐ 5.   The man-made elements.

☐ 6.   A group (a group runs up and down the chart).

☐ 7.   The elements of the very last period (the bottom row) are radioactive. Locate these radioactive elements. In addition to this group of radioactive elements, there are some radioactive elements scattered throughout the chart.

☐ 8.   Locate H - Hydrogen. This is a gas, not a metal. Hydrogen, atomic number 1, is an exception. Write the name for each symbol.

TEACHER CHECK _____ _____
                                          initials   date

Match these items.

2.1 _____ smallest particle of an element

2.2 _____ anything that takes up space and has mass

2.3 _____ chemical elements that are located on the left side of the stairs on the Periodic Table

2.4 _____ a method of comparing atomic weights to carbon

2.5 _____ elements of the last period on bottom of the chart

2.6 _____ a material that takes the shape of its container

2.7 _____ a substance whose molecules consist of atoms that are united chemically

a. atom

b. metals

c. nonmetals

d. matter

e. liquid

f. compound

g. relative weight

h. radioactive substances

Complete these activities.

2.8 Write the symbol for each of the following elements.

a. potassium _____   b. sodium _____   c. tin _____

d. iron _____   e. zinc _____   f. fluorine _____

g. helium _____   h. carbon _____   i. chlorine _____

j. calcium _____   k. hydrogen _____   l. sulfur _____

m. silver _____   n. gold _____

2.9 Write the name for each of the following symbols.

a. Cu _____   b. Mg _____   c. N _____

d. P _____   e. U _____   f. Si _____

g. Ni _____   h. Co _____   i. Pb _____

j. O _____   k. Ca _____   l. K _____

2.10 Diagram the carbon atom in the space below.

LIGHT

Light from the sun travels by *waves*. It also may travel by energy packets known as *photons*. It can travel through space or in a vacuum, which has no air. Many forms of radiation reach the earth from the sun and other stars. Visible light is only a tiny portion of the radiation that strikes the earth. Cosmic rays, X-rays, and ultraviolet light are a few examples of invisible radiation. The visible and invisible radiation collectively are called the *electromagnetic spectrum*.

The speed of light. In the air, light travels at approximately 186,000 miles per second. In glass it travels at about two-thirds this rate. Light normally travels in a straight line. Its rays are bent when passing from one substance to another. This bending of light is called *refraction*.

Transmission. A *transparent* material is one that is clear and allows light to pass through it. Clear glass, air, water, and clear plastics are transparent. A *translucent* material is one that allows some light to pass through it. Examples of translucence are frosted or colored glass and parchment paper. An *opaque* material is one that does not allow any light to pass through it. Shadows are cast by opaque objects.

| Refraction of light

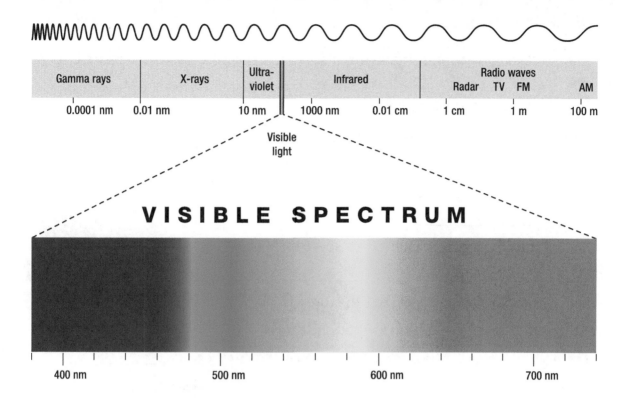

VISIBLE SPECTRUM

400 nm   500 nm   600 nm   700 nm

The spectrum. In 1672, Sir Isaac Newton found that white light could be separated into a band of colors. By passing light through a prism, he was able to separate light into the colors of the rainbow. The band of colors that light is separated into is called the *spectrum*. The colors of the spectrum are always in the same order. Red is the longest wavelength; violet the shortest. The colors in order of appearance are red, orange, yellow, green, blue, indigo, and violet. Sunlight or white light is a mixture of these colors.

The rainbow. When light is refracted in raindrops, a rainbow is formed. The raindrop acts like a prism and refracts the light until you can see the colors of the rainbow.

Colors. Colors are visible only when objects reflect light. If you awaken early in the morning, just before daylight, things will be shades of gray, black, and white. No colors are seen in the dark. An object appears colored if light is reflected. A green dress reflects green. Black absorbs light. For example, a piece of black cloth will appear black, even if you look at it through colored glass. The color of an object depends upon which color of the spectrum is reflected.

Mixing colored lights and mixing colorants do not produce the same results. The three primary colors of the light spectrum are red, green, and blue. Other colors of light are produced by mixing the primary colors. A mixture of the primary colors of light produces white light. If you were to flash red, green, and blue light onto a screen and mix them together, they would produce white light. When you mix red and green light, it produces yellow light. Remember, this process is not the same as mixing colorants.

When you mix colorants, such as paints or crayons, you are mixing pigments. The results are quite different from those obtained by mixing light. The primary colors of pigments are red, yellow, and blue. Mixing red and yellow produces orange; yellow and blue make green; red and blue make violet. These new colors of orange, green, and violet are the secondary colors. By mixing various combinations of pigments or dyes, an artist can achieve a desired color.

Review. If you do not understand this discussion, review Section 3 of Science LIFEPAC 606.

Complete the following activities.

2.11 List the colors of the spectrum, beginning with the shortest wave length.

a. _____   b. _____   c. _____

d. _____   e. _____   f. _____

g. _____

2.12 What are the primary colors of the light spectrum?

a. _____   b. _____   c. _____

2.13 What color do you get when you mix the three primary colors of light? _____

2.14 What color do you get when you mix red and green light? _____

2.15 An object will appear as the color it reflects. A red dress reflects _____ .

2.16 What is the speed of light in the air? a. _____ miles per b. _____ .

2.17 What are the primary colors of pigments?

a. _____   b. _____   c. _____

2.18 Mixing red and yellow pigments make a. _____ ; yellow and blue make

b. _____ ; and red and blue make c. _____ .

2.19 Three general types of material may be defined according to their transmission of light.

Material that is clear and allows light to pass through it is called a. _____ .

Material that allows some light to pass through it is called b. _____ .

Material that will not allow any light to pass through it is called c. _____ .

Write these words on a whiteboard : *Electromagnetic Spectrum.*

2.20 With your classmates or a friend or a parent try to see who can make the most words from these two words. The one who finds the most words in ten minutes is the winner.

Write the words you have made in this space.

_____

_____

_____

_____

_____

SOUND

All sounds are produced by vibrations. When you strike a drum or cymbal, the object vibrates. These vibrations set air molecules into motion. Sound waves move away from their source. They travel on air molecules. When the vibrating air molecules reach your ear, the eardrum also vibrates. The bones of the ear vibrate in the same manner as the object that started the sound wave. These vibrations enable you to hear different sounds. Even musical tones are vibrations. Irregular vibrations are noise.

Compression, rarefaction. Sound waves have two parts: *compression* and *rarefaction*. Compression describes the part of the waves where the molecules of air are pushed (compressed) together. Rarefaction describes the part of the waves where the molecules are far apart. Sound waves are a series of compressions and rarefactions.

The speed of sound. Sound waves can travel through liquids, solids, and gases. They can travel through water faster than through air. They travel even faster in solids such as stone, iron, and steel. Sound travels 1,100 feet per second (about one-fifth of a mile) in the air.

Pitch and amplitude. *Pitch* describes the highness or lowness of sound. Pitch is determined by the number of vibrations per second. The highest key on a piano vibrates 4,000 times per second. Middle C vibrates 256 times per second. The loudness of a sound is its *amplitude*. Striking a key harder will make it louder. It will not change the pitch.

Review. If you have difficulty with this discussion on sound, review Section 1 of Science LIFEPAC 606.

Match these items.

2.21 _____ the loudness of a sound

2.22 _____ the source of all sound

2.23 _____ describing a sound as high or low

2.24 _____ middle C on the piano

2.25 _____ the part of a sound wave where molecules of air are pushed together

2.26 _____ sound travels through this medium faster than through air

2.27 _____ the speed of sound

2.28 _____ the part of a sound wave where molecules of air are far apart

a. pitch

b. vacuum

c. about 1/5 mile per second

d. amplitude

e. rarefaction

f. compression

g. 256 vibrations per second

h. solids

i. vibrations

MOTION

Everything in the world is made of *matter*. All matter is in motion. The atoms and molecules that make up matter are in constant motion. The electrons move around the nucleus. The protons and neutrons within the nucleus are also in motion. A force is required for movement. Force is defined as a push or a pull action.

Work. Scientists define *work* in a special way. Work is done only when a force moves something. If you attempted to move an object and were unable to do so, you did no work. You exerted a force and spent some energy, but did not accomplish anything. Work is defined as the amount of force times the distance the force moves.

The unit for measuring work is the foot-pound. If you move 2 pounds 1 foot, you have done 2 foot-pounds of work. Also, if you have moved 10 pounds 2 feet, you have done 20 foot-pounds of work. The formula for computing work is:

WORK (foot-pounds) =

FORCE (pounds) x DISTANCE (feet)

In the metric system, the unit for measuring work is the kilogram-meter. When a kilogram weight is raised to a height of 1 meter, 1 kilogram-meter of work is done. Also, when 3 kilograms are lifted 2 meters, 6 kilogram-meters of work are done.

The scientific definition of *power* is the rate or speed of an energy force doing work. Suppose Sue weighs 90 pounds. Sue climbed to the top of a 10-foot stairway in 3 seconds. Mary also weighs 90 pounds, but it took her 6 seconds to climb the same stairway. Sue's power is twice that of Mary's. Notice that both girls have done the same amount of work. Only the rate (power) has changed. (Note: This example only measures the work required to move vertically up the steps and does not measure the work required to move horizontally on the steps. Since the work required to move vertically is much greater than that required to move horizontally in this example, it is approximately the same as the total work required.)

The unit of measuring power is the *horsepower*. Horsepower is defined as the power required to lift a 550-pound load 1 foot in 1 second. Electrical power is measured in watts. Watts are much smaller units than horsepower. One horsepower has 746 watts. Watts are useful measurements for small engines and household items such as vacuum cleaners.

Machines. A *machine* is a mechanical device people use to help them do work. Machines help people do work with less force or in less time. They do not reduce the amount of work to be done. They can save a lot of effort. More work is needed to operate a machine because of *friction*. Friction is a force that opposes motion. It is a hindrance to work because parts move against one another. Friction is necessary when walking on the pavement and when stopping your car. If the road is icy, friction is decreased. Without friction, you could not stand up. Although friction is useful for standing and stopping and other similar things, it causes a problem in operating machines.

Scientists have found that the work output of a machine equals the work put into a machine. This principle is known as the work principle. Not all of the work from a machine is useful, because some may be lost as heat or friction. Machines are very helpful to man because they can transfer a force and also change the direction of a force. Machines, such as the turbine, are used for generating power. The turbine is an example of a machine that can change the direction of a force. When you push down on your bicycle pedal, you change the direction of a force and your bicycle goes forward.

Review. If you have difficulty with this discussion on motion and its measurement, review Science LIFEPAC 607.

Complete the following activities.

2.29 Solve this problem. How much work was done when 70 pounds were moved 10 feet? _____ (indicate units)

2.30 Solve this problem. How much work was done when 7 kilograms were moved 2 meters? _____ (indicate units)

2.31 Define *power*. _____

2.32 What is the work principle? _____

2.33 What is friction and how does it hinder machines? _____

_____

_____

2.34 Explain why lack of friction on a highway can be dangerous. _____

_____

_____

TEACHER CHECK _____ _____
initials date

Review the material in this section in preparation for the Self Test. This Self Test will check your mastery of this particular section as well as your knowledge of the previous section.

SELF TEST 2

Match these items (each answer, 2 points).

2.01	_____ the loudness of sound	a. geotropism
2.02	_____ a by-product of photosynthesis	b. atom
2.03	_____ the rate of doing work	c. power
2.04	_____ the smallest particle of an element	d. vein
2.05	_____ a method of comparing atomic weights	e. amplitude
2.06	_____ the name of the vascular bundle in a leaf	f. yellow
2.07	_____ a substance whose molecules consist of atoms that are chemically united	g. pitch
		h. oxygen
2.08	_____ a response to gravity	i. compound
2.09	_____ the quality of a sound, describing it as high or low	j. blue
2.010	_____ the color produced by a mixture of red and green light	k. relative weight
		l. vascular cylinder

Complete the following activities (each answer, 2 points).

2.011 Write the chemical symbol for each of the following elements.

a. potassium _____   b. helium _____

c. hydrogen _____   d. fluorine _____

e. sodium _____   f. sulfur _____

g. chlorine _____   h. calcium _____

2.012 Write the name for each of these chemical symbols.

a. Ca _____   b. N _____   c. Mg _____

d. Co _____   e. U _____   f. Cu _____

g. K _____   h. P _____   i. Pb _____

j. O _____   k. Si _____   l. Ni _____

Answer true or false (each answer, 2 points).

2.013 _____ Substances found to the left of the stairs on the Periodic Table are metals.

2.014 _____ Radioactive substances are the last period of elements (on the bottom of the chart).

2.015 _____ The major function of the large intestine is absorption of food.

2.016 _____ A mutation is a change in a gene that is transmitted to offspring.

2.017 _____ Red is the shortest wave of the visible spectrum.

2.018 _____ Colors are made only when objects reflect light.

2.019 _____ The tundra biome does not have trees.

2.020 _____ Mixing red and yellow pigments produces orange.

2.021 _____ Bile breaks down fats and aids in digestion.

2.022 _____ Friction hinders work, but it is necessary for walking.

2.023 _____ When 10 pounds are moved 10 feet, 100 foot-pounds of work are done.

2.024 _____ Carl Correns devised the Punnett Square.

2.025 _____ Light travels slower through glass than it does through air.

2.026 _____ Auxin is a natural plant regulator.

Complete the following activities (each answer, 6 points).

2.027 Briefly describe the electromagnetic spectrum. _____

_____

_____

_____

_____

2.028 Briefly describe a sound wave and how it travels. _____

_____

_____

_____

_____

80/100   SCORE _____   TEACHER _____ _____
initials   date

3. SPACESHIP EARTH AND THE STARS

As you have seen in the first two sections of this LIFEPAC, God has designed our earth and universe in remarkable ways through plants and animals, the laws of chemistry and physics, and the other things that He has made. In this section of the LIFEPAC, you will review the motion of "spaceship earth" as it travels in several ways through the Universe. In addition, you will review the wonders of our Solar System and the stars that God has made.

Section Objectives

Review these objectives. When you have completed this section, you should be able to:

10. Describe the various motions of earth.

11. Name and describe the various parts of our Solar System.

12. Identify important people, events, and observing equipment in the history of astronomy.

13. Describe how stars differ and identify some of their main characteristics.

Vocabulary

Review the vocabulary words in Science LIFEPACs 608 and 609.

Study this word to enhance your learning success in this section.

emit (i mit). To send out.

Pronunciation Key: hat, āge, cãre, fär; let, ēqual, tèrm; it, īce; hot, ōpen, ôrder; oil; out; cup, pút, rüle; child; long; thin; /ŦH/ for then; /zh/ for measure; /u/ or /ə/ represents /a/ in about, /e/ in taken, /i/ in pencil, /o/ in lemon, and /u/ in circus.

EARTH'S ROTATION

The earth makes one complete turn on its axis every twenty-four hours. It rotates west to east. This produces the effect of the sun rising in the east and setting in the west. The earth's speed of rotation is about 1,040 miles per hour at the equator. Further north or south of the equator, its speed is less because the distance around the earth is smaller. The length of day and night changes because the axis on which the earth rotates is tilted toward the plane of its orbit around the sun.

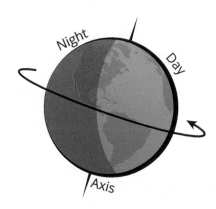

Earth's tilt on its axis. The earth's axis is tilted approximately 23.5°. The major cause of the changes in seasons and the length of days is the Earth's tilt on its axis. This tilting causes the polar regions to receive six months of continuous darkness and six months of continuous daylight. When it is dark at the North Pole, it is light at the South Pole. In the temperate zones, we are aware of long summer days and the short winter days.

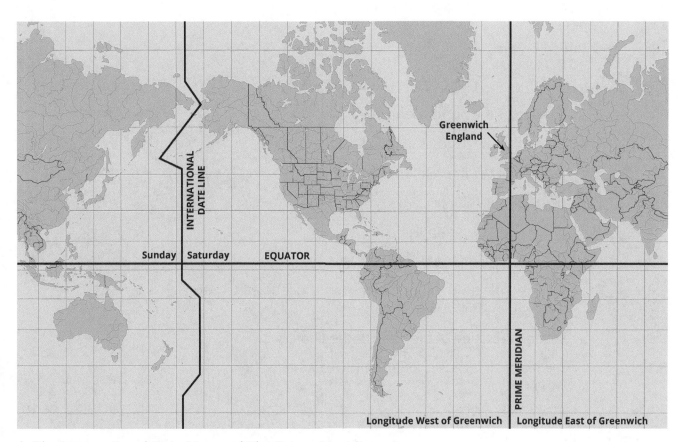

| The International Date Line and The Prime Meridian

Time. In relation to the sun, the earth makes one revolution about its axis in 24 hours. This is called a *solar day*. Since the path around the equator is a circle, there are 360° around the earth. Therefore, it is convenient to divide the earth into time zones. 360° divided by 24 hours = 15°. The earth rotates 15° per hour. The imaginary lines that divide the earth every 15° are called *meridians*. They are also lines of *longitude*. They extend from pole to pole. Therefore, the earth is subdivided into twenty-four time zones consisting of 15° each called *standard time*.

The *prime meridian* is located at 0° longitude. Exactly one-half of the way around the earth from there, at 180° longitude, is the *International Date Line*. By agreement with other nations, the International Date Line is where the new day begins. The International Date Line runs from north to south through the Pacific Ocean. In order to avoid dividing a land mass, it zigzags through the Pacific Ocean.

The contiguous United States has four time zones. These are Eastern, Central, Mountain, and Pacific time zones. They do not exactly follow the lines of longitude. They zigzag around heavily populated areas in order to avoid dividing cities. The zones listed above are in order, beginning with the east and going to the west.

 Match these items.

3.1	_____ the amount of tilt of the earth on its axis	a. standard time
3.2	_____ location of the prime meridian	b. 180°
3.3	_____ the number of degrees in a circle	c. six months
3.4	_____ location of the International Date Line	d. 1,040 mph
3.5	_____ degrees longitude per time zone	e. 360°
3.6	_____ time of darkness at poles	f. Pacific
3.7	_____ the time zone of the U.S. West Coast	g. 0°
3.8	_____ an agreement with other nations to divide the earth into twenty-four time zones	h. 23.5°
		i. 15°
3.9	_____ speed of rotation of the earth at the equator	j. central
3.10	_____ the factor that causes long summer days and short winter days	k. mountain
		l. tilt of the earth

EARTH'S ORBIT

The earth orbits around the sun in approximately 365 days. Because it does not take exactly 365 days, one full day is added to the calendar every fourth year. This day is added to the month of February. The year in which this occurs is called a *leap year*. Whenever your calendar indicates 29 days for February, you have a leap year that year!

Elliptical orbit. The orbit of a heavenly body is its curving pathway in space. Earth's orbit is an *ellipse*. An ellipse is an oval-shaped orbit. All of the planets in our Solar System have orbits that are ellipses. Spacecraft also have elliptical orbits.

The earth does not follow a straight line as it moves through space. Its pathway is curved because of the pull of gravity. Gravity is the force that holds the earth in its orbit. The earth continues to move in its orbit around the sun because of inertia. Inertia does not explain how it started moving. Inertia merely states that a moving body continues to move in a straight line unless acted upon by another force. Gravity is that unbalanced force that causes it to move in a curved path.

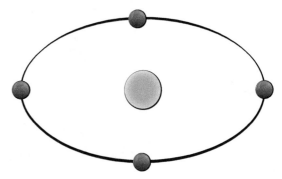

The Earth Has an Elliptical Orbital Around the Sun

| The earth has an elliptical orbit around the sun.

The seasons. The orbit of the earth around the sun and the earth's tilt on its axis cause the seasons. Because of this tilt, days and nights are equal on about March 21. This date is called the *vernal* (or *spring*) *equinox*. During the summer the days are long. On about September 22, day and night again become equal. This time is called the *autumnal equinox*. The longest day of the year is about June 21 and the shortest is about December 22.

✏️ **Complete the following statements.**

3.11 The orbit of the earth around the sun takes approximately _____ days.

3.12 An orbit is _____ .

3.13 The two major causes of the seasons are a. _____ and

b. _____ .

3.14 The longest day of the year is about a. _____ ; the shortest day is about

b. _____ .

3.15 What is the equinox? _____

_____

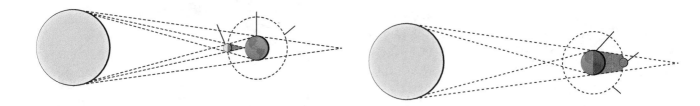

| Comparison of a solar eclipse (left) and a lunar eclipse (right)

ECLIPSES OF THE SUN AND MOON

An *eclipse* is the darkening of one heavenly body by another. The eclipse of the sun is called a *solar eclipse*. The eclipse of the moon is called a *lunar eclipse*. One of the best ways to distinguish between a solar and a lunar eclipse is to refer to the meaning of the word eclipse. Eclipse means the darkening of a heavenly body. During a lunar eclipse, the moon is darkened because of the earth's shadow. During a solar eclipse, the sun is darkened because of the moon blotting it out.

Solar eclipse. When the moon passes between the earth and the sun, the moon's shadow falls on the earth causing a solar eclipse. Since the moon is small compared to the earth, only a small portion of the earth will see a solar eclipse. The darkest part of the shadow is called the *umbra*. The lightest part of the shadow is called the *penumbra*. A partial eclipse is seen in the penumbra.

Lunar eclipse. An eclipse of the moon, a lunar eclipse, occurs when the earth passes between the moon and the sun. Because the moon is so small compared to the earth, the entire moon may lie within the umbra. A full eclipse is seen in the umbra.

Complete the following statements.

3.16 Describe a solar eclipse. Be sure to include the positions of the sun, moon, and earth.

_____

_____

_____

3.17 Describe a lunar eclipse. Be sure to include the positions of the sun, moon, and earth.

_____

_____

_____

OUR SOLAR SYSTEM

Spaceship earth is part of our Solar System. The solar system consists of the sun, the eight major planets, dwarf planets, asteroids, comets, and meteoroids—meteors and meteorites that have not entered earth's atmosphere. Some important information about these objects is given in this part of the LIFEPAC.

The sun. The sun is composed primarily of hydrogen and helium gases. A trace of other elements have also been identified as part of the sun's make-up. The energy source for the sun is *nuclear fusion*, where hydrogen is turned into helium with the release of tremendous amounts of light and heat energy. The sun's surface temperature is estimated at 10,000 degrees Fahrenheit.

The sun has a central core, which is the place where most of its power is generated. In this region, hydrogen is fused to form helium.

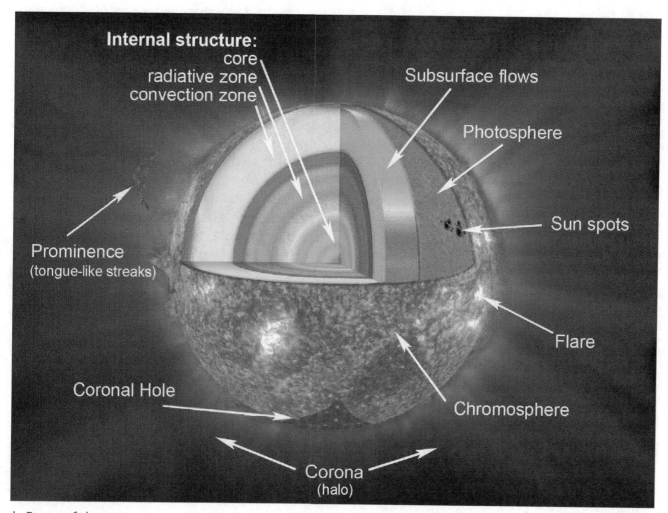

| Parts of the sun

Moving outward from the core, the next layer is one of hot, glowing gases known as the *photosphere*. This layer is the visible surface of the sun. Above the photosphere is another layer of brilliant, red gases known as the *chromosphere*. Just above the sun's surface is a halo known as the *corona*. The corona is seen only during an eclipse. Streams of hot gases streak out into space from the sun, sometimes for millions of miles. These streams of hot gases are called *prominences*.

The surface of the photosphere sometimes shows dark spots. These spots are known as *sunspots*. They appear to be magnetic disturbances. They occur in an eleven-year cycle, with a greater cycle consisting of twenty-two years. Just outside of the darker spots are bright spots called *solar flares*. Solar flares release enormous amounts of energy and charged particles. Showers of protons and electrons bombard the earth about twenty-six hours after the appearance of solar flares. Solar flares also **emit** X-rays and cosmic rays.

When charged particles from the sun are captured by earth's magnetic field, a brilliant glow results, usually near the earth's poles. The night sky may be streaked with green, blue, white, and red. Green is usually the major color. This display of lights is known as the *northern lights* in the northern hemisphere, or the *aurora borealis*. In the southern hemisphere, it is called the *southern lights*, or the *aurora australis*.

Planets. Our solar system contains eight major planets. In order from the sun outward, they are Mercury, Venus, Earth, Mars, Jupiter, Saturn, Uranus, and Neptune. Pluto is dwarf planet on the outer edge of the solar system. It has an unusual orbit. Every 248 years, Pluto's orbit goes inside the orbit of Neptune, making Neptune farther away from the sun than dwarf planet Pluto for about 20 years. This was the case from January 23, 1979 through March 15, 1999. Now, dwarf planet Pluto is once again outside Neptune's orbit and is farther from the sun.

Mercury is the smallest planet and Jupiter is the largest. The most unusual characteristics about planet earth are its oxygen, water, and climate, which make it suitable for life.

Planets glow by reflected light. Unlike the sun or stars, they do not produce light of their own. Venus is often referred to as the "morning star" because it brilliantly reflects the light of the sun toward earth. Although they do not produce their own light, most of the planets that we can readily see from earth are very bright. Venus is almost the brightest object in the morning and evening sky. Mars does not glow as brightly, but it does have a distinctive red color.

Asteroids, comets, and meteoroids. Our Solar System has numerous other bodies. *Asteroids* are small planet-like objects. In fact, they are sometimes called minor planets. There are thousands of asteroids in our Solar System, most of them orbiting the sun between Mars and Jupiter. *Comets* are groups of particles consisting of rock, metals, and frozen gases. *Meteoroids* are smaller particles of dust and rock that do not enter the earth's atmosphere. If they enter earth's atmosphere, they begin to glow as they burn up from the friction against the atmosphere. Then they are called *meteors* or "shooting stars." Sometimes, meteors are large enough to hit the earth. Those that do are called *meteorites*.

Match these items.

3.18	_____	the sun's energy	a. aurora borealis
3.19	_____	the northern lights	b. aurora australis
3.20	_____	dark areas on the sun	c. solar flares
3.21	_____	a source of charged particles that hit the earth	d. sunspots
3.22	_____	the visible surface of the sun consisting of a layer of hot glowing gases	e. prominences
			f. corona
3.23	_____	the halo around the sun	g. central core
3.24	_____	streaks of hot gases that go out into space a million or more miles	h. photosphere
			i. chromosphere
3.25	_____	the layer above the photosphere that consists of brilliant red gases	j. fusion of hydrogen
3.26	_____	the southern lights	

Complete the following statements.

3.27 Planets do not have light of their own. They glow by _____ light.

3.28 The planet closest to the sun is _____ .

3.29 The largest planet is _____ .

3.30 Earth is very special and unusual because of the conditions that support life. Some of these special characteristics are a. _____ , b. _____ , and c. _____ .

3.31 An asteroid is like a small _____ .

3.32 Comets are _____

_____ .

3.33 A shooting star is what we call a _____ .

3.34 A meteorite is a _____ .

3.35 The planet called "the morning star" is _____ .

BRIEF HISTORY OF ASTRONOMY

The study of the stars and other objects in the universe is called *astronomy*. It is one of the oldest sciences. The Chinese, Greeks, and Babylonians observed the stars and made observations about them in the time before Christ (B.C.). Ptolemy, a Greek astronomer living in the second century A.D., held the view that the sun circled around the earth. His ideas were accepted for almost 1500 years, up to the time of a Polish astronomer, Nicolaus Copernicus. In 1543 A.D., Copernicus proposed that the sun was the center of the solar system and that the earth and other planets revolved around the sun. Modern astronomy can be dated with the ideas of Copernicus in the 16th century.

In the early 17th century, Galileo Galilei, an Italian astronomer, developed the *refracting telescope* for use by astronomers. With it, he saw craters and mountains on the moon. He discovered four of Jupiter's moons, saw that Saturn had rings, and observed the phases of the planet Venus as it orbited around the sun.

| An early refracting telescope

He also observed sunspots on the sun and determined that the Milky Way had individual stars. Later in the 17th century, Isaac Newton, an Englishman, made important contributions

| The Hubble Space Telescope

to astronomy. He invented the *reflecting tele-scope*, discovered the law of gravitation, and discovered that visible light can be broken down into a *spectrum*.

In the 18th, 19th, and 20th centuries, new planets were discovered in the solar system. William Herschel discovered Uranus in 1781, and Johann Galle discovered Neptune in 1846. In 1930 Clyde Tombaugh, an American astrono-mer, discovered the dwarf planet, Pluto.

In the first half of the 20th century, other new discoveries were made that advanced the science of astronomy. In 1905 and 1915, Albert Einstein developed *theories of relativity* that changed the way we understand energy, mass, space, and time. In 1929, an American astron-omer, Edwin Hubble, demonstrated that the universe is expanding. In 1931, Karl Jansky, an American engineer, discovered radio waves coming from the center of the Milky Way Gal-axy. A few years later, Grote Reber, an amateur

astronomer, designed a *radio telescope* and began to use it to detect radio waves from outer space. Since then, very large radio telescopes have been built at locations around the world.

With the launch of the Russian artificial satellite, Sputnik, in 1957, a new era in space exploration began. Astronomy has advanced greatly in this "space age." Unmanned space observatories and probes have been sent to distant planets and other bodies in our Solar System. In 1990, the Hubble Space Telescope was launched. It has revealed much greater details about parts of our universe than were possible from earth-based optical telescopes. In 1999, the Chandra X-ray Observatory was launched and promises to give even more detail than the Hubble Space Telescope. New, more powerful earth-based telescopes were also developed during the last part of the 20th century. Astronomy is one of the most exciting of sciences, not only for pro-fessionals, but for amateur astronomers as well.

Match these items.

3.36 _____ Ptolemy

3.37 _____ Copernicus

3.38 _____ Galileo

3.39 _____ Newton

3.40 _____ Hubble

3.41 _____ Jansky

3.42 _____ Grote Reber

3.43 _____ Einstein

3.44 _____ Sputnik

3.45 _____ Chandra

a. developed theories of relativity

b. discovered the universe is expanding

c. built first radio telescope

d. X-ray observatory

e. first artificial satellite

f. said sun revolved around earth

g. said earth revolved around sun

h. used refracting telescope to discover four of Jupiter's moons

i. invented reflecting telescope and discovered law of gravitation

j. discovered radio waves from space

THE STARS

Stars are different from each other. Stars range in size from giants to dwarfs. Their size and distance from earth make them look bright or dim to us. The temperature of a star gives it a characteristic color. Cool stars appear red; very hot stars appear white. Each element in a star gives off a different colored line in a spectrum. The elements that make up a star can be identified by breaking up its light into a spectrum and looking at the dark lines. Helium, an element that hydrogen is converted into during the process of nuclear fusion in a star, was discovered in a spectrum before it was discovered on earth.

Color and temperature. Stars display a wide variety of colors. Colors are interpreted as temperature differences. The hotter the star, the greater its brightness. The hottest stars are the giant blues. The coolest ones are dwarf reds. Our sun is a medium-sized star, which is yellow in color. Star colors, temperature, and brightness are all associated. Light from a star can be separated into colors and analyzed for lines which identify the elements present. Dark lines in the spectrum, called *Fraunhofer lines*, identify elements in the star's cooler atmosphere.

Giants and dwarfs. Most stars can be measured only by indirect methods. Their sizes have been a puzzle. The smallest stars are dwarf white stars. Giant red stars have always posed a problem. It was once thought that giant reds were stars that were contracting. Now it is believed that giant reds are older stars that are expanding.

Our sun is approximately halfway between the giants and dwarfs in size. It is considered a medium sized star. The diameter of the sun is about 864,000 miles. It is about 1 million times larger than the volume of the earth!

Review Section 2 of the Science 609 LIFEPAC on "The Stars," and especially note the part on "Elements and Spectra." To help you review this information, place a check mark in the box after you have completed each step.

Complete this assignment.

☐ 1. Review how the spectrum of a star aids in its study.

☐ 2. Be able to explain the meaning of Fraunhofer lines.

☐ 3. Note how helium was discovered.

MAGNITUDE AND LUMINOSITY

The brightness of a star is called its *magnitude*. The modern brightness scale can list numbers that are negative for some of the brightest objects in the heavens. The brighter the star, the higher its negative number. For example, Sirius is magnitude -1.6; the sun is -26.7. Most stars have a positive magnitude number. The lower the number, the brighter the star. The limit to the naked eye is about a magnitude 6 star. This magnitude scale describes how bright a star appears to an observer on earth. It is called *apparent magnitude*. The apparent magnitude can be misleading as to the actual brightness of a star. A very bright star that is very far away can appear dim to us on earth. True, or real, luminosity, is called *absolute magnitude*. It is a more accurate estimate of the actual brightness of a star.

Complete the following statements.

3.46 Stars differ in a. _____ , b. _____ , c. _____ ,

and d. _____ .

3.47 The brightness of a star is called its _____ .

3.48 The sun is a _____ -sized star.

3.49 Fraunhofer lines are _____

_____ .

3.50 Helium was first discovered _____ .

3.51 The study of a star's spectrum helps to identify _____ .

3.52 The hottest stars are _____ .

3.53 The coolest stars are _____ .

Answer the following question.

3.54 Why can apparent magnitude be a misleading number? _____

_____

_____

TEACHER CHECK _____ _____

initials   date

Before you take this last Self Test, you may want to do one or more of these self checks.

1. _____ Read the objectives. See if you can do them.
2. _____ Restudy the material related to any objectives that you cannot do.
3. _____ Use the **SQ3R** study procedure to review the material:
  a. **S**can the sections.
  b. **Q**uestion yourself.
  c. **R**ead to answer your questions.
  d. **R**ecite the answers to yourself.
  e. **R**eview areas you did not understand.
4. _____ Review all vocabulary, activities, and Self Tests, writing a correct answer for every wrong answer.

SELF TEST 3

Match these items (each answer, 2 points).

3.01	_____	the color produced by a mixture of red and green light
3.02	_____	the loudness of sound
3.03	_____	a response to light
3.04	_____	cell division in which the new cells have the same number of chromosomes as the parent cells
3.05	_____	an important function of the small intestine
3.06	_____	an important function of the large intestine
3.07	_____	organisms that fix nitrogen on legumes
3.08	_____	the name of plant tubes that transport food
3.09	_____	openings on the underside of a leaf
3.010	_____	a by-product of photosynthesis
3.011	_____	a liquid waste eliminated from the blood
3.012	_____	a substance whose molecules consist of atoms that are chemically united
3.013	_____	the location of metals on the Periodic Table
3.014	_____	the rate of doing work
3.015	_____	the complex chemical that transmits traits
3.016	_____	the time of the year when the days and nights are equal
3.017	_____	the visible surface of the sun
3.018	_____	the color of the hottest stars

a. power
b. left side of the stairs
c. right side of the stairs
d. absorb water
e. absorb food
f. bacteria
g. DNA molecule
h. amplitude
i. urine
j. phototropism
k. photosphere
l. yellow
m. bluish-white
n. oxygen
o. compound
p. mitosis
q. phloem
r. element
s. stomata
t. equinox

Answer true or false (each answer, 1 point).

3.019 _____ The differences in the colors of the stars are interpreted as temperature differences.

3.020 _____ Isaac Newton developed the refracting telescope.

3.021 _____ The 3 most distant planets in our Solar System were discovered in the 17th century.

3.022 _____ Radioactive substances are located on the top period of the Periodic Table.

3.023 _____ A study of the spectrum of the sun led to the discovery of helium.

3.024 _____ Fusion of hydrogen is the main source of the sun's energy.

3.025 _____ A solar flare may cause charged particles to enter the earth's atmosphere.

3.026 _____ Apparent magnitude refers to the actual luminosity of a star.

3.027 _____ The tilt of the earth on its axis is a major cause of the seasons on earth.

3.028 _____ The corona is the halo of light around the sun; it consists of gases.

3.029 _____ The clavicle is a leg bone.

3.030 _____ The gastrocnemius is a muscle found in the leg.

Complete the following statements (each numbered answer, 3 points).

3.031 Three ways that stars differ are a. _____ , b. _____ , and c. _____ .

3.032 Studying the Fraunhofer lines helps to identify _____ on the stars.

3.033 The simplest particle of an element is an _____ .

3.034 The sun is the brightest star to earth because _____ .

3.035 Our sun's surface temperature is approximately _____ .

3.036 One of the main functions of the skin is to cool the body. This cooling is done by _____ .

3.037 Bile produced by the gall bladder is important in the breakdown of _____ .

3.038 Photosynthesis takes place primarily in the _____ .

3.039 A biome is _____ .

Write the symbols (each answer, 1 point).

3.040 Write the chemical symbol after each chemical listed.

　　a. potassium ＿＿＿＿＿　　b. iron ＿＿＿＿＿　　c. sodium ＿＿＿＿＿

　　d. nickel ＿＿＿＿＿　　e. carbon ＿＿＿＿＿

Complete the following activities (each answer, 5 points).

3.041 Distinguish between a solar and a lunar eclipse.

＿＿＿＿＿＿＿＿＿＿＿＿＿＿＿＿＿＿＿＿＿＿＿＿＿＿＿＿＿＿＿＿

＿＿＿＿＿＿＿＿＿＿＿＿＿＿＿＿＿＿＿＿＿＿＿＿＿＿＿＿＿＿＿＿

＿＿＿＿＿＿＿＿＿＿＿＿＿＿＿＿＿＿＿＿＿＿＿＿＿＿＿＿＿＿＿＿

＿＿＿＿＿＿＿＿＿＿＿＿＿＿＿＿＿＿＿＿＿＿＿＿＿＿＿＿＿＿＿＿

3.042 Briefly tell how the study of the sun's spectrum is important.

＿＿＿＿＿＿＿＿＿＿＿＿＿＿＿＿＿＿＿＿＿＿＿＿＿＿＿＿＿＿＿＿

＿＿＿＿＿＿＿＿＿＿＿＿＿＿＿＿＿＿＿＿＿＿＿＿＿＿＿＿＿＿＿＿

＿＿＿＿＿＿＿＿＿＿＿＿＿＿＿＿＿＿＿＿＿＿＿＿＿＿＿＿＿＿＿＿

＿＿＿＿＿＿＿＿＿＿＿＿＿＿＿＿＿＿＿＿＿＿＿＿＿＿＿＿＿＿＿＿

3.043 Briefly tell how the lungs obtain oxygen for body cells.

＿＿＿＿＿＿＿＿＿＿＿＿＿＿＿＿＿＿＿＿＿＿＿＿＿＿＿＿＿＿＿＿

＿＿＿＿＿＿＿＿＿＿＿＿＿＿＿＿＿＿＿＿＿＿＿＿＿＿＿＿＿＿＿＿

＿＿＿＿＿＿＿＿＿＿＿＿＿＿＿＿＿＿＿＿＿＿＿＿＿＿＿＿＿＿＿＿

＿＿＿＿＿＿＿＿＿＿＿＿＿＿＿＿＿＿＿＿＿＿＿＿＿＿＿＿＿＿＿＿

3.044 Distinguish between a natural plant regulator and an artificial one.

＿＿＿＿＿＿＿＿＿＿＿＿＿＿＿＿＿＿＿＿＿＿＿＿＿＿＿＿＿＿＿＿

＿＿＿＿＿＿＿＿＿＿＿＿＿＿＿＿＿＿＿＿＿＿＿＿＿＿＿＿＿＿＿＿

＿＿＿＿＿＿＿＿＿＿＿＿＿＿＿＿＿＿＿＿＿＿＿＿＿＿＿＿＿＿＿＿

＿＿＿＿＿＿＿＿＿＿＿＿＿＿＿＿＿＿＿＿＿＿＿＿＿＿＿＿＿＿＿＿

80/100　　**SCORE** ＿＿＿＿＿　　**TEACHER** ＿＿＿＿＿ ＿＿＿＿＿
　　　　　　　　　　　　　　　　　　　　　　initials　　date